MYRANDA WALTER

COLLEGE KNOWLEDGE

**The Ultimate Guide to Choosing a Community College,
Learn All the Information About How to Pick a Community College
That Would Be Best For You**

Descrierea CIP a Bibliotecii Naţionale a României
MYRANDA WALTER
  COLLEGE KNOWLEDGE. The Ultimate Guide to Choosing a Community College, Learn All the Information About How to Pick a Community College That Would Be Best For You / Myranda Walter – Bucharest: Editura My Ebook, 2020
  ISBN

MYRANDA WALTER

COLLEGE KNOWLEDGE

**The Ultimate Guide to Choosing a Community College,
Learn All the Information About How to Pick a Community
College That Would Be Best For You**

My Ebook Publishing House
Bucharest, 2020

TABLE OF CONTENTS

TABLE OF CONTENTS

CHAPTER 1

INTRODUCTION TO COMMUNITY COLLEGE

In order to obtain the right place for your ultimate learning experience, choosing community college is considered as one of the salient factors that you should take into account. It is true that choosing a reliable and competent Community College is not an easy task since it requires time, effort, dedication and passion to make sure that you will come up with positive outcomes you deserve to have.

In order to choose a community college that will perfectly suit with your budget, desire and field of interest, here are some of the valuable tips that you may follow on how to choose the right option to consider:

Tips on how to Choose the precise Community College

After you graduated from high school, the next thing you need to ponder on is to find out the proper community college that will provide you with ultimate learning experience that you really want to get. Seeking out for a proficient community college is the first step towards achieving your set goals in life. If you and your family can't afford the tuition rate in other private institutions and universities, choosing community college must be your ideal option. In order for you to perfectly opt to the elite community college within your society, the following tips are highly recommended.

Visit the website of your chosen Community College or Request for a Catalog

This is the first thing is that you need to do to find out the programs and classes offered by such community college and foresee their offered courses that will catch your attention and interests.

Plan for an appointment with their School Counselor

When you already set an appointment with their school counselor, this is the best time for you to tackle the skill and field of your interests. A school counselor will greatly help you pick the appropriate courses that will suit your skills and abilities. Moreover, the school counselor is also the one who will discuss the financial aid and answer all your questions, concerns and queries.

Learn about the Job Opportunities and Placement Services

Grab the opportunity to find out if your chosen community college offers job assistance and placement services. You are also required to conduct research about your chosen community college if they already provided their graduates with job assistance. You can also ask them if they offer internships and hands-on trainings.

Ask for Financial Aid

This is also one of the salient factors you need to consider in choosing a community college. You need to ask them about financial aid application especially when it comes to transportation availability since the financial aid will greatly help you with your financial needs.

Check out the Class Schedule

If you are working, it is highly recommended to check out the schedule of their classes that will not conflict your working schedule. If not, you need to talk with their supervisor if they will let you work around the school schedule.

Find out if they offer Extracurricular Activities

The existence of extracurricular activities will depend on the community college. There are community colleges that offer school publication and student clubs where you can join. Furthermore, there are also social activities and sports team that a certain community college offer to their potential students.

CHAPTER 2

BENEFITS OF COMMUNITY COLLEGE

The community college is considered as one of the optimum places wherein you can easily knock out and explore general courses that will suit with your field of interest. It is true that a community college will greatly help you to immediately figure out the degree that you really want to pursue.

There are various benefits that you will get from entering a community college and it is very important that you are aware about those valuable benefits. The following are some of the integral benefits of a community college that you must learn and know more about. Discover the real benefits of it and rest assured that you will be astonished with those facts.

The Integral Benefits of Community College

In choosing the correct community college for your ultimate learning experience, it is very imperative that you are also aware about the amazing benefits that it will offer you. A competent and consistent community college will provide you with essential benefits that you are seeking for. Here are some of them:

Tuition Cost

It is a fact that tuition cost is one of the reasons why most students choose to study in a community college since it has affordable tuition fee as well as it is a financial advantage to those students who can't afford to attend in private learning institutions and famous Universities. According to researches, most community colleges that are available today offer low tuition fees for about 2,000 dollars every semester. Moreover, the community college will give you a chance to easily prepare the financial issues and demands of a 4-year course.

Flexible Schedule

If you are one of those students who are planning to work while you are studying, the community college is the ideal option that is best for you. Most of the community colleges offer night classes and a wide variety of schedule options to choose from. When it comes to workload, you don't need to worry since it is lighter compared to private institutions and state schools. The best thing about community college is that attendance is not totally required.

Give the students the opportunity to discover their major options If you are not yet sure about the major course you want to take up, studying at a community College is the right thing you should do. In order to avoid spending too much of your money for private universities for a certain major, a community college will greatly help you come up with the elite decision. A community college will give you a great chance to discover your interests and your chosen field of specialization.

Smaller Classes

Most community colleges have a maximum of 20 students in each class than the universities. In this way, the professors have the chance to explore the abilities and capabilities of their students. Most of the students of a community college can easily focus on their chosen courses since they have smaller classes. If ever they need assistance from their professors, they can easily access ask for it anytime.

Qualified Professors

A community college is very flexible not just for those students but also for the professors. Most qualified professors edify a part time job at a community college to pursue their career goals.

CHAPTER 3

CHOOSING COMMUNITY COLLEGE THROUGH COURSES AVAILABLE

In order to make sure that you will attain the right place for your ultimate learning experience, you need to choose a Community College that offers courses that suit your desire and field of interest.

Before selecting a community college, it is very important that you know the courses that they are offering to their students and this is one of the reasons why conducting a research to your chosen community college is highly recommended.

The following are the facts you need to know and learn about choosing the course that is available in a certain community college.

Facts about Choosing the Available Courses at Community College

Most community colleges will offer their students with various courses that they will surely love. However, it is not advisable to immediately opt to a certain community college without knowing the courses they offer in the first place. It is very imperative that you know their available courses to make sure that you have chosen the right place for your learning experience.

Course Scheduling

When you finally choose your desired course, the next thing you need to do is to know the schedule of the classes. It is also very important that you are aware about the courses' schedule to make sure that you will be able to attend your classes on time. If your field of interest is to be a teacher, you need to find a community college that offers education courses. It simply means that you need to evaluate first the course you want to take up before choosing any community college.

Course Selection

The course selection will depend on the student. You can also seek out for a community college and ask them about the courses they are offering to their students and if you are interested with their offered courses, this is the best time for you to know more about the evaluation options, course requirements and degree alternatives.

Pre-Requisites

When you hear the term "pre-requisites", what is the first thing that comes into your mind? Well, it simply means that pre-requisites are the requirements or course conditions that you need to meet before you can enroll in your chosen course. Most of the community colleges will not allow any students to enroll without completing the pre-requisites.

Corequisites

It is a kind of course that must be simultaneously taken. For example, the CHEM101 must be concurrently taken with MATH120. As a student of a community college, you are required to comply with the rules and guidelines regarding the courses offered.

Course Syllabus

It is a copy of a certain syllabus for every course that is being offered by the community college that will also serve as the reference of the students. You need to make sure that the community college that you choose can provide your desired course.

Course Format

Most of the professors at a community college are required to distribute the course format to their students. It usually contains valuable information about the teaching methods, evaluation criteria, instructional materials and pertinent organization. Select the right community college that will offer you with your preferred course of interest.

CHAPTER 4

PICK COMMUNITY COLLEGE
WITH FINANCIAL SUPPORT

Are you one of those students who can't afford the tuition rates of other leading universities and private institutions? Then, picking a community college with financial support is the ideal option that you should ponder on. In this way, you can be sure that the school will help you with your financial problems and issues so that you can finish your studies.

According to researches, there is a community college that offers financial assistance to their students and this is one of the reasons why most students today decide to study at a community college. The following are the top reasons why you need to pick a community college that offers financial support to students.

The Top Reasons why you need to pick Community College with Financial Support

It is true that most families today are suffering from extreme poverty and this is one of the reasons why they don't have the ability to send their children to college. However, with the existence of a community college that provides financial support, they will greatly help you support the financial needs of your children in college.

Support Services

Most of the community colleges will offer their students with support services such as library services, financial aid, health care, tutorials, advising and counseling. There are also computer laboratories that will help the students to easily complete their assignments and projects. In this way, you will not find a hard time and difficulty about your college expenses since the community college will greatly help you resolve your financial needs.

Affordability

The annual fees and tuition at a community college is about 2, 402 dollars which is relatively cheaper compared to 6,

585 dollars of most private universities. Furthermore, you can also live in the comfort of your home and you can save on food and housing expenses. In order to reduce your college expenses, the community college will provide you with financial aid, work study and part time jobs you will surely love.

Convenience

Most of the community colleges will also offer locations and class hours that are suitable for all students. The classes are being offered during weekends, evening class and off campus. At a community college, you can freely opt to attend the classes on either part time or full time basis.

Open Access

Most community colleges don't have an admittance standard that usually requires high grades and test scores on the college admission test. If you have your high school diploma, you are very welcome to enroll. Attending the classes at a community college will give you a chance to easily improve your records before you decide to transfer from a university.

Teaching Quality

Most of the professors in a community college have an apparent understanding about student learning and teaching. Moreover, the community college is also accredited by agencies of major universities. Apart from support services, a community college will provide you with various financial services that will greatly help you attain your set goals in life in just a short period of time.

In choosing a community college, the first thing that you should take into consideration is the one that will offer you with financial aid and support services that are worth looking for.

CHAPTER 5

GO WITH COMMUNITY COLLEGE
WITH JOB ASSISTANCE

In choosing a community college, there are some factors that you need to consider to make sure that you will choose the right community college that will greatly help you obtain your ultimate learning experience. One of the important factors that you should ponder on is to find a community college that will provide you with job assistance.

Today, there are various community colleges that offer different courses for you to opt from. However, you need to make sure that the community college you choose will also offer you with job placement and assistance after you graduate.

In this way, you can be sure that they will help and assist you until you find the job that will be suitable with your educational attainment. The following are the benefits that you will experience when you choose a community college that offers job assistance.

The Amazing Benefits of Choosing Community College with Job Assistance

In order to make sure that you will completely obtain the ultimate learning experience, a community college that offers job assistance and placement is the perfect choice for you. It is very important that you carefully choose a community college since not all of them can offer job assistance to anyone. When you finally found a community college that will provide you with excellent job assistance, here are some of the exceptional benefits that you will experience:

Higher Wages

When you already receive your degree, it simply means that you will not find a hard time and difficulty in finding a job that is related to your chosen field of specialization. At the same time, your chosen community college will help you seek a high paying job.

Job Advancement and Skill Building

A competent and reliable community college will also offer you with courses that will suit your interest and your specific needs for personal development, job placement and job advancement. If your academic performance is great, your chosen community college will refer you to a certain reputable organization or they can hire you to be part of their institution.

Strong Foundation

A community college that will offer you with job assistance can also provide you with programs and developmental courses that will help you build strong foundation before you graduate. It simply means that you will have a great edge to others since you are completely ready to face the new chapter of your life which is to seek a job and getting hired. When you have a strong foundation, there are different employers and organization that will offer you with various job opportunities.

Explore Options

A community college will allow you to discover different options and areas of your interests before you choose your area of specialization. They will serve as your guide to make sure that you will never have regrets from your chosen course. When they notice that you are performing your well in your studies, there is a great chance that they will choose to make you a part of their family or they can also refer you to other organizations where you can get a high paying job.

CHAPTER 6

CHECKING OUT COMMUNITY COLLEGE
REVIEWS ONLINE

Before attempting to enroll in a community college, the first thing you need to do is to check out some of the reviews on their website. Most students are disappointed to find that they have chosen the wrong community college so in order to avoid this scenario; it is very important that you visit their website and conduct your own research about the background of your prospect community college.

The reputation of a certain community college is highly recommended and you need to make sure that they possess a good record especially when it comes to the courses that they are offering to their students as well as the programs that they are implementing.

Most community colleges have their own website so you will not find a hard time and difficulty to find out some of the reviews of your desired community college. The following are the things you need to know about a community college.

Things you need to know about Community College

When you decided to check out their website and foresee some of the community college reviews, the first thing you should take into account is the reputation and years of service of your preferred school. In order for you to have a clear and better understanding with this, here are some of the salient things you need to know about a community college.

- An effective community college offers the students a chance to easily save money, be ready for their career and enjoy a flexible schedule.

- According to researches, 44% of undergraduate students are studyng at a community college since they believe that it will serve as their gateway to experience the ultimate learning experience.

- In choosing for a consistent community college, you need to check first the years of their service and the reputation status of a certain learning institution in order to make sure that they have a vast knowledge and expertise in executing their courses offered and the programs implemented.

- The revenues of a community college derived from the local industry and business, contracts and gifts, local appropriations, federal, state, fees and tuition.

- A community college will also provide the students with broad associate and certificate degree programs that will help them seek for a job that is related with their chosen course.

- Most of the degree programs that are being offered by a community college include business management, religion, philosophy and health professions. You can be sure that most community colleges will offer you with course and programs that you desire.

- Furthermore, you also need to know if a certain community college already helps the students in their job assistance programs and financial support programs.

CHAPTER 7

VISITING THE COMMUNITY COLLEGE
ON OPEN DAY

If you are planning to visit a community college, the best time to do it is during weekdays and preferably in the morning. In this way, you can be sure that the faculty and staff of the school are present during office hours.

When you visit a community college, it is very important that you are aware about the factors you need to tackle with their community college staff. In order for you to be familiar with this, the following are some of the essential factors you need to be aware of.

The Salient Factors that you must be aware about Visiting Community College

In visiting a community college, there are salient factors that you really need to consider in order to make sure that you know all the important details in choosing a community college as well as to easily obtain the ultimate learning experience that you are searching for. When you visit a community college during the open days, you can be sure that you will be properly entertained by the staff of a community college as well as you will know the salient things you need to know about a community college.

You can be familiar with their Academic Programs

Most community colleges are open during weekdays and morning is the best time to visit them since most of them accept the college applicants in the morning. In this way, you will have a great chance to know the academic programs and courses that are being offered by your desired community college.

You will also know the Student Diversity

The community college will vary on college population diversity and most of the community colleges offer student breakdown by student diversity and geographic location. When you decided to visit a community college, this is one of the salient factors that you must be aware of.

The Ratio of Female and Male Students

This is one of the important things that you need to know in visiting a community college. This is also one of the advantages of visiting a community college during open days since all your questions and queries about the courses that they usually offer can be answered completely.

You will also explore the Campus Life

In visiting a community college, it is very imperative to know some of the organized activities and events that they are offering to their students that may include the religious organizations, cultural organizations, music club, community service, action clubs, academic clubs, honor societies, magazines, school publications, campus media and student government.

Cost

This is the most salient factor that you need to know when you visit a community college. You need to inquire about the tuition fee of your chosen course. In attending your classes at a community college, the cost include miscellaneous expenses, transportation, personal expenses, supplies and books, activity fees and course tuition. However, you don't need to worry since there is also a community college that offers financial support to their students that will greatly help them to budget their money wisely.

CHAPTER 8

SEARCHING COMMUNITY COLLEGE WITH GREAT LOCATION

One of the elite factors that you should take into consideration in choosing for a community college is the great location that is accessible to your home. Apart from the tuition, choosing the great location on your desired community college is one of the significant things to ponder on.

The location of your chosen community college is also one of the major concerns of most parents and it is highly recommended to consult your parents about this matter. The following are some of the integral benefits that you will experience in choosing for a great location on your chosen community college.

The Essential Benefits in Choosing for a Great Location of Community College

It is true that most of the parents want their children to choose a community college that is within their community. A community college that is within your community will greatly help save money from the rising transportation cost. Instead of spending your money in your transportation expenses, you can make use of it in other important projects in your studies.

- When your chosen community college is located just within your locality, you will not find a hard time and difficulty in traveling a long way just to go home on time.

- If you are attending your college life in a community college, you will be able to prevent distractions like hanging out with your friends. Usually in big towns, there are different party towns that will hinder your focus on your studies.

- A great location of your chosen community college will also help you to focus more on your academics effectively and seek for some of the extracurricular activities that will also greatly help you obtain the ultimate learning experience that you deserve to have.

- In order to completely save your transportation allowance, you can just walk from your home to school particularly if your chosen community college is just a few steps away from your home. In this way, you can be sure that you can immediately save money from your allowance.

CHAPTER 9

UNDERSTANDING THE SOCIAL NETWORKING
IN COMMUNITY COLLEGE

Today, most community colleges are still hesitant to make use of social media in their respective premises. It is true that a community college is one of the most extremely significant parts of higher education and it has unique needs and only the existence of social media can addressed the problem.

Since most community colleges are uncertain to invest their resources on this new medium, the following are the top reasons why the presence of social media is completely precise for them.

The Top Reasons why Social Media is Right for Community College

Most of the students in a community college are definitely active on their respective social media sites. It is true that most of the social networking sites have the ability to help the students perform their daily activities effectively. Here are some of the top reasons why social media is right for a community college:

- According to researches, most of the students in a community college are extremely active and using social media sites. LinkedIn, Pinterest, Google+, Twitter and Facebook are few of the top visited social networking sites that are widely used by most students in a community college.

- A social networking site will greatly help those students to share their experiences, interest and explore your identity. Moreover, the students of a community college need social support and connections to foster social connections and relationships. The temperament of social networking site is to enable those students to easily connect with one another.

- The social networking sites have the potential to provide an outlet to share questions and obtain different answers from their fellow students. In order to disseminate the important information of the community college, you can easily reach the student body through email, Facebook notification, iPhone notification and text message.

CHAPTER 10

DECIDE IF COMMUNITY COLLEGE IS FOR YOU

Determining if a certain community college is right for you is not an easy task. There are various factors you should consider before you will come up with a great decision.

However, with comprehensive research and better understanding in choosing a community college, you can be sure that choosing the best community college that will suit with your personality, needs, wants and desires can be a great help. The following are some of the salient factors in choosing and deciding if a community college is the best for you.

The Salient Factors in Choosing and Deciding if Community College is best for you

In order to easily attain the ultimate learning experience, choosing the elite community college can be a great help. It is very imperative that you decide if a community college is the best for you, however, you need to consider several factors to make sure that you will come up with a great decision.

- You will immediately notice that a certain community college is the best for you if they provide you with top notch instructors and professors with utmost track records and excellent academic achievements.

- An effective community college will provide their students with financial incentives and merit scholarships grant that will greatly help you save money for future use.

- The best community college will offer you with exceptional curriculum and course work that will serve as your guide and key in attaining your set goals in life.

When you follow all the valuable information that are stated within this book, you can be sure that choosing the best community college will become an easy task for you to deal with. Always remember that obtaining the ultimate learning experience is the elite part of being a community college student.

Printed by Libri Plureos GmbH in Hamburg,
Germany